AF265896

THE BÁB AND BAHÁ'U'LLÁH
The Twin Manifestations of God

Written and Illustrated by Melissa López Charepoo

All rights reserved.

No part of this book may be reproduced, stored in a
retrieval system, or transmitted in any form or by any means, electronic,
mechanical, photocopying, recording, or otherwise, without the prior
written permission of the publisher.

Text and Illustrations
© 2020 Melissa López Charepoo

First published 2020. Reprint 2026.

ISBN 978-1-971750-14-9 (paperback)

Why are the Báb and Bahá'u'lláh called the "Twin Manifestations of God"?

God has made a Covenant, or pact, with humanity to never leave us without His loving guidance. From time to time, God sends Divine Messengers -also called Prophets or Manifestations of God- to reveal His message to humanity. This concept is called the Progressive Revelation of God.

The Báb and Bahá'u'lláh were both Manifestations of God. They founded Their own religions - the Bábí Faith and the Bahá'í Faith - and revealed Their own sacred writings. Usually Messengers are sent hundreds of years apart, yet the Báb revealed His mission only a few years before Bahá'u'lláh revealed His. The purpose of the Báb's short Dispensation was to prepare humanity for the coming of an even greater Manifestation of God than Himself, "Him Whom God shall make manifest." This prophecy was fulfilled in the person of Bahá'u'lláh.

So unified are their Dispensations that Bahá'u'lláh has said about the anniversaries of Their births:
"These two days are accounted as one in the sight of God."
- Bahá'u'lláh, *The Kitáb-i-Aqdas*

In this book you will find facts and milestones of the lives of the Báb and Bahá'u'lláh in a format that is easy to compare and contrast.

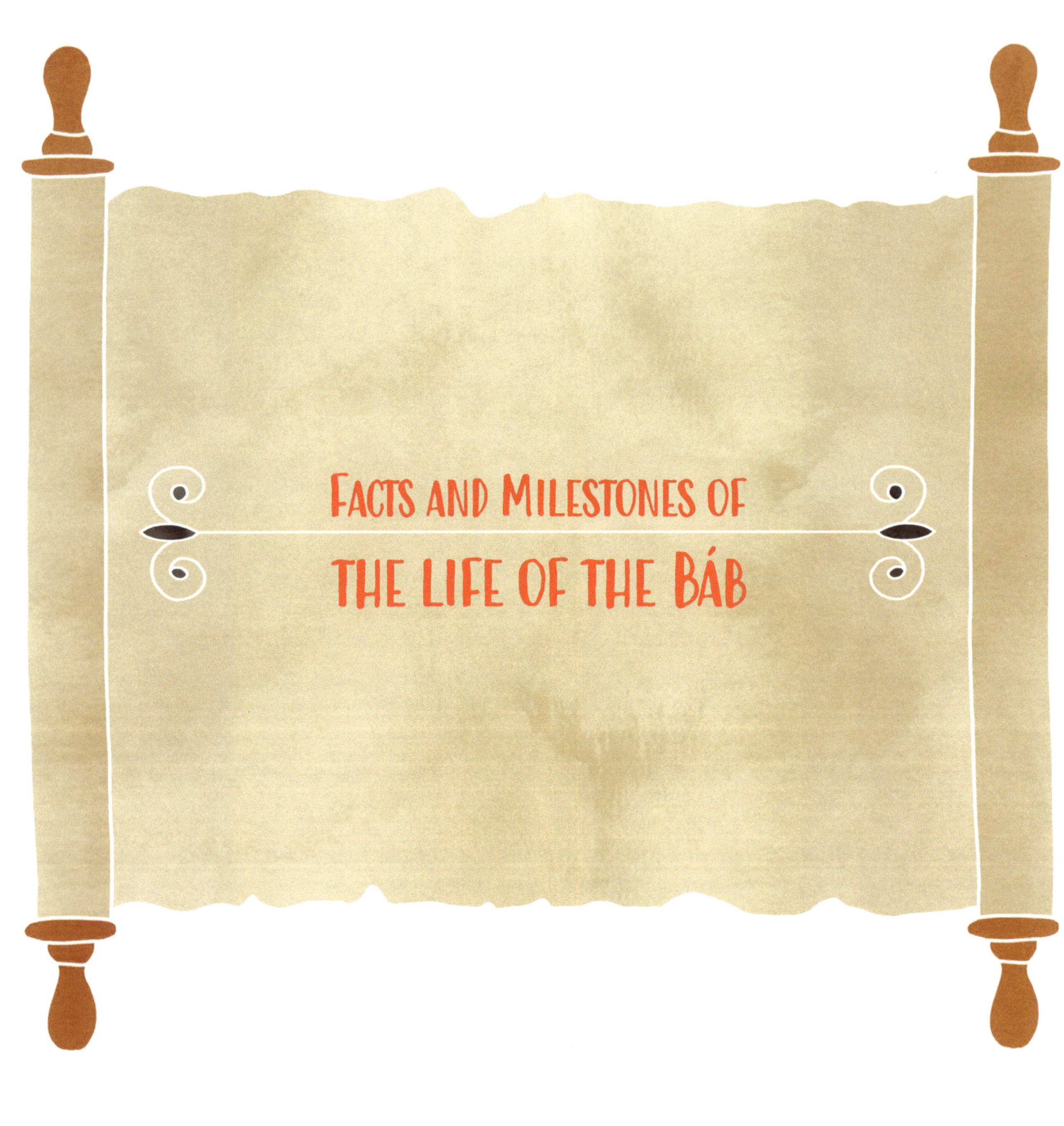

Facts and Milestones of
the Life of the Báb

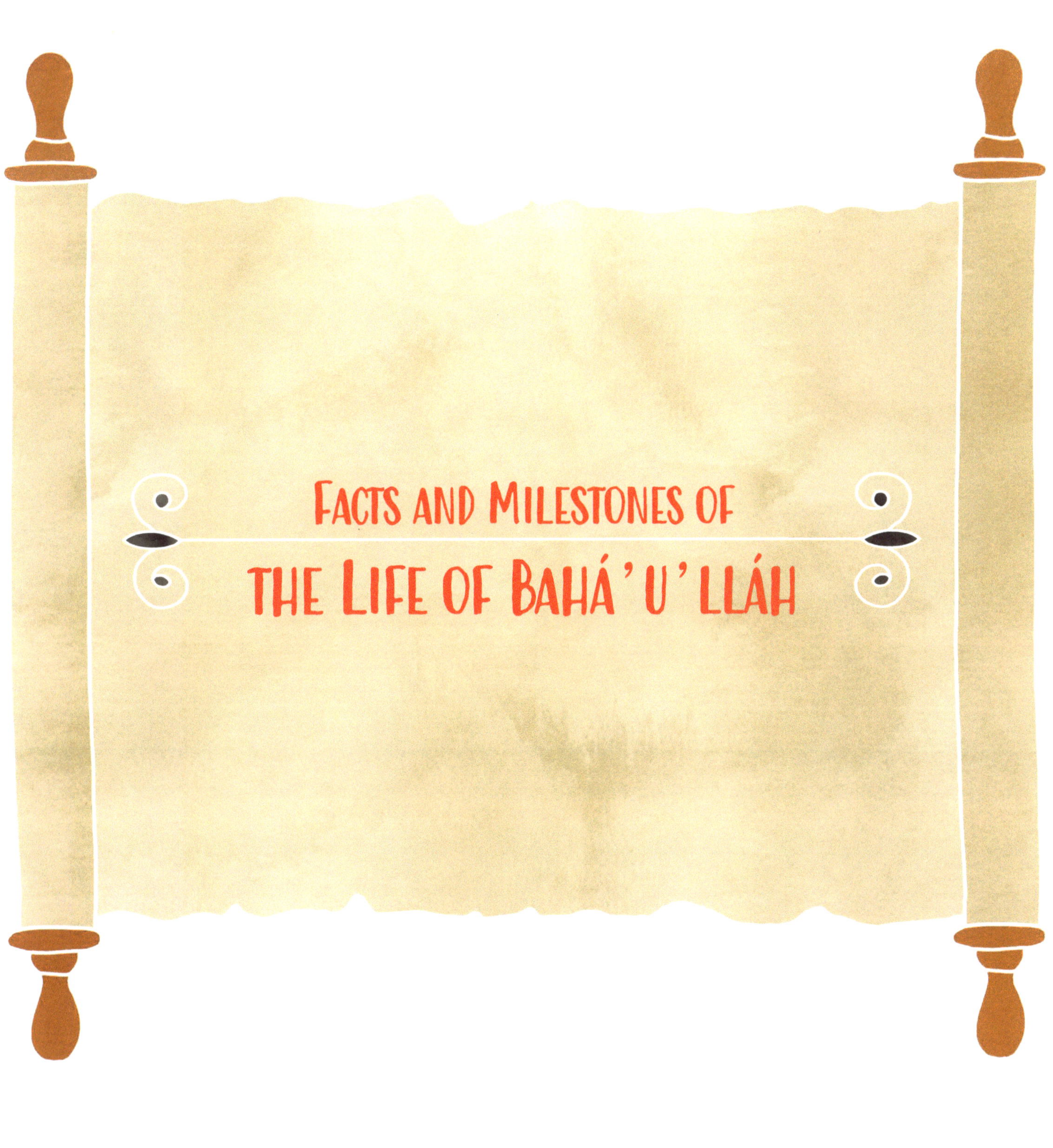
FACTS AND MILESTONES OF
THE LIFE OF BAHÁ'U'LLÁH

The Birth of the Báb

1 Muḥarram	Ṣafar	Rabi'-I	Rabi'-II
Jumada-I	Jumada-II	Rajab	Sha'ban
Ramadan	Shawwal	Zul-Qi-dah	Zul-Hijjah

The Báb was born on the first day of Muḥarram 1235 A.H. of the Islamic calendar. The date was equal to October 20th, 1819, on the Gregorian calendar.

The Birth of Bahá'u'lláh

Hijri Islamic Calendar 1233 A.H.

2 Muḥarram	Ṣafar	Rabi'-I	Rabi'-II
Jumada-I	Jumada-II	Rajab	Sha'ban
Ramadan	Shawwal	Zul-Qi-dah	Zul-Hijjah

Bahá'u'lláh was born on the second day of Muḥarram 1233 A.H. of the Islamic calendar. The date was equal to November 12th, 1817, on the Gregorian calendar. This was two years before the birth of the Báb but a day later in the month.

The Birth Place of the Báb

The Báb was born in the city of Shíráz, Persia.

The Birth Place of Bahá'u'lláh

Bahá'u'lláh was born in the city of Ṭihrán, Persia.

The Ancestry of the Báb

The Báb was a descendant of the Prophets Abraham and Muḥammad.

The Ancestry of Bahá'u'lláh

Bahá'u'lláh was a descendant of the Prophets Abraham and Zoroaster, and of the Sasanian Kings of Persia.

THE PARENTS OF THE BÁB

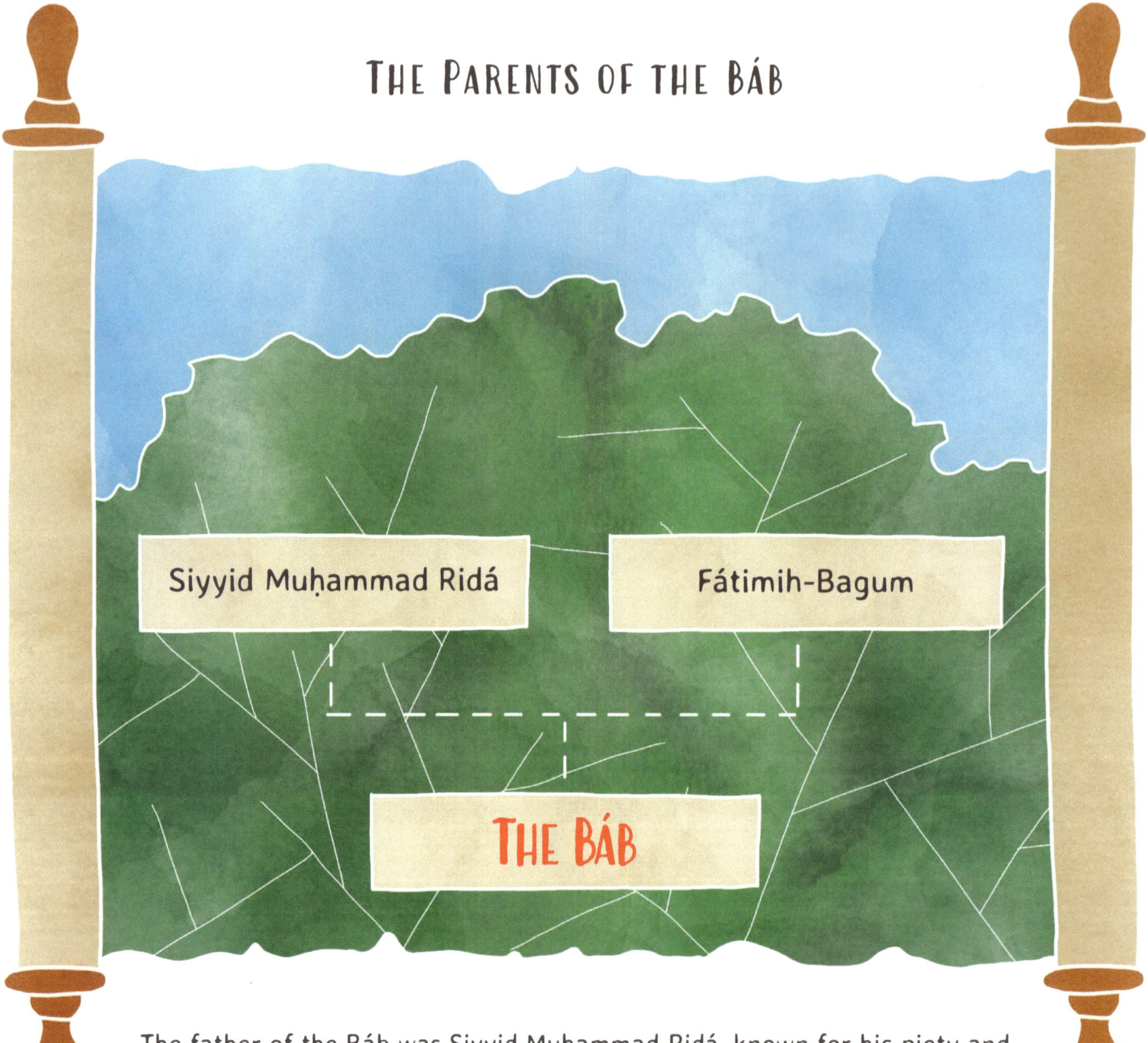

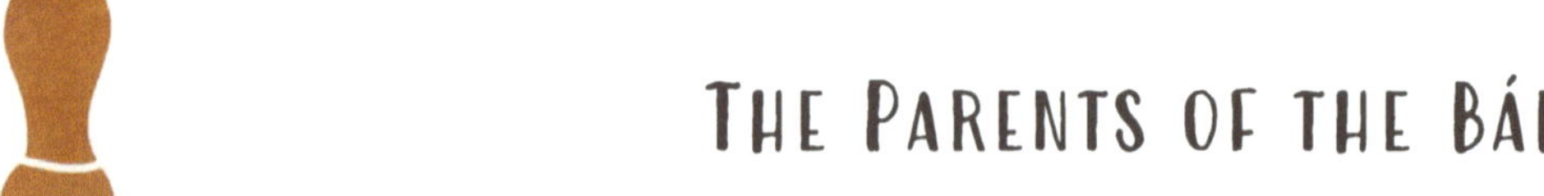

The father of the Báb was Siyyid Muḥammad Riḍá, known for his piety and virtue. His mother was Fáṭimih-Bagum, a member of a prominent merchant family of Shíráz.

The Parents of Bahá'u'lláh

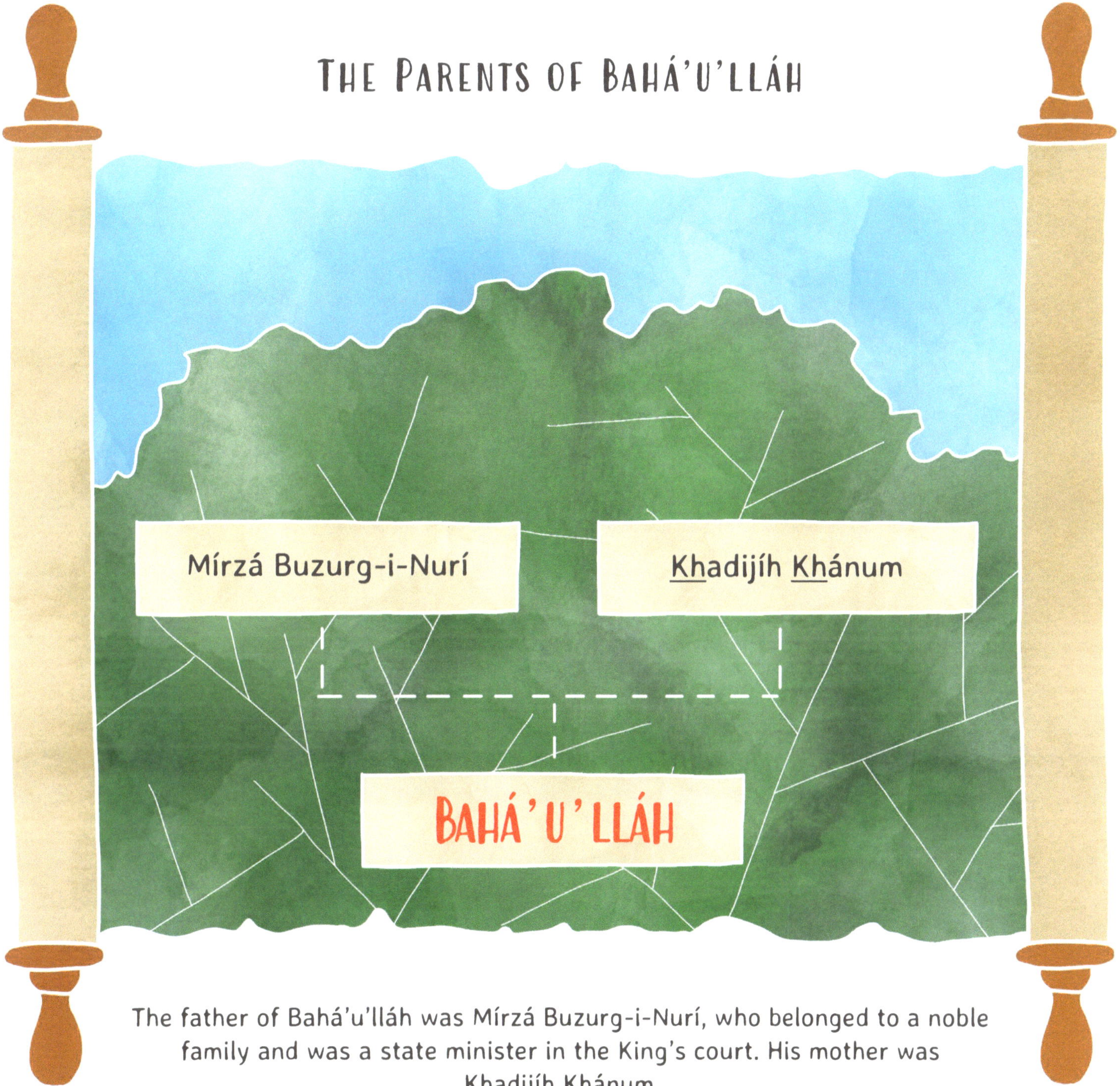

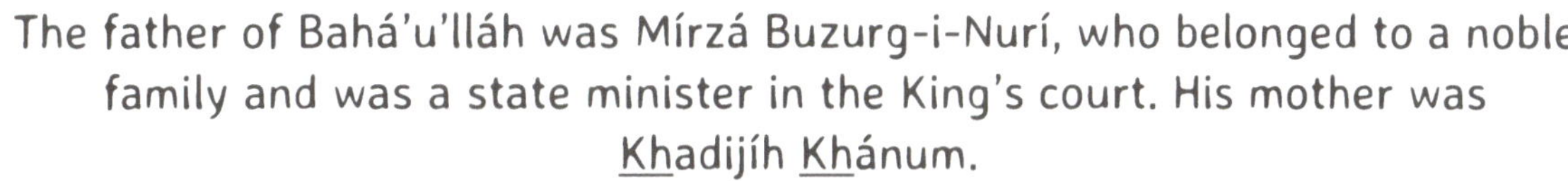

The father of Bahá'u'lláh was Mírzá Buzurg-i-Nurí, who belonged to a noble family and was a state minister in the King's court. His mother was Khadijíh Khánum.

THE GIVEN NAME OF THE BÁB

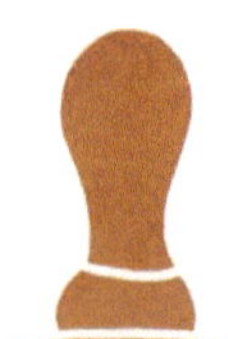

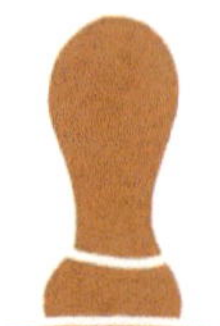

SIYYID 'ALÍ MUḤAMMAD

The Báb's given name was Siyyid `Alí Muḥammad.
The title "Siyyid" was a sign that He was a descendant of the Prophet Muḥammad.

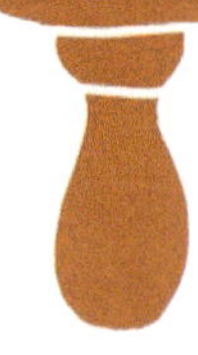

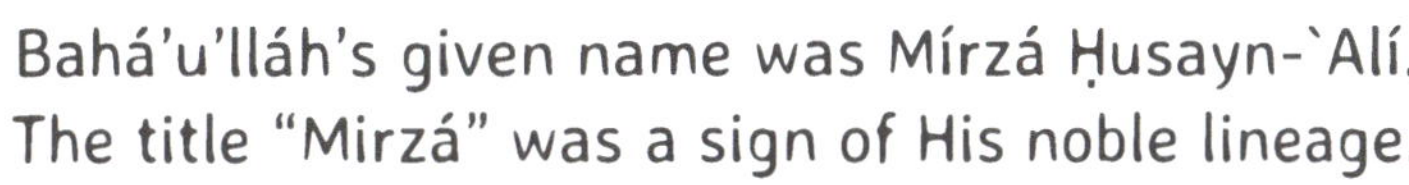

Bahá'u'lláh's given name was Mírzá Ḥusayn-ʻAlí.
The title "Mirzá" was a sign of His noble lineage.

The Head Covering of the Báb

The Báb wore a green turban – a long piece of cloth wrapped around a cap – as a sign that He was a descendant of the Prophet Muḥammad.

The Head Covering of Bahá'u'lláh

Bahá'u'lláh wore a táj – a tall felt hat - as a symbol of His station as a Manifestation of God.

The Title of the Báb

The title "the Báb" means "the Gate."
The Báb took His title during His declaration to Mullá Ḥusayn in 1844.

The Title of Bahá'u'lláh

The title "Bahá'u'lláh" means "Glory of God."
Bahá'u'lláh took His title during the conference of Bada<u>sh</u>t in 1848.

The Báb as a Child

As a child, the Báb was gentle, humble, and serene. He showed signs of greatness and knowledge that only come from God. Indeed, His teacher at school felt inadequate to teach Him.

BAHÁ'U'LLÁH AS A CHILD

As a child, Bahá'u'lláh was very well mannered, kind, and thoughtful. Like most children of noble families, Bahá'u'lláh did not attend formal school; yet, from a young age, Bahá'u'lláh showed signs of innate knowledge inspired by God.

The Báb as a Youth

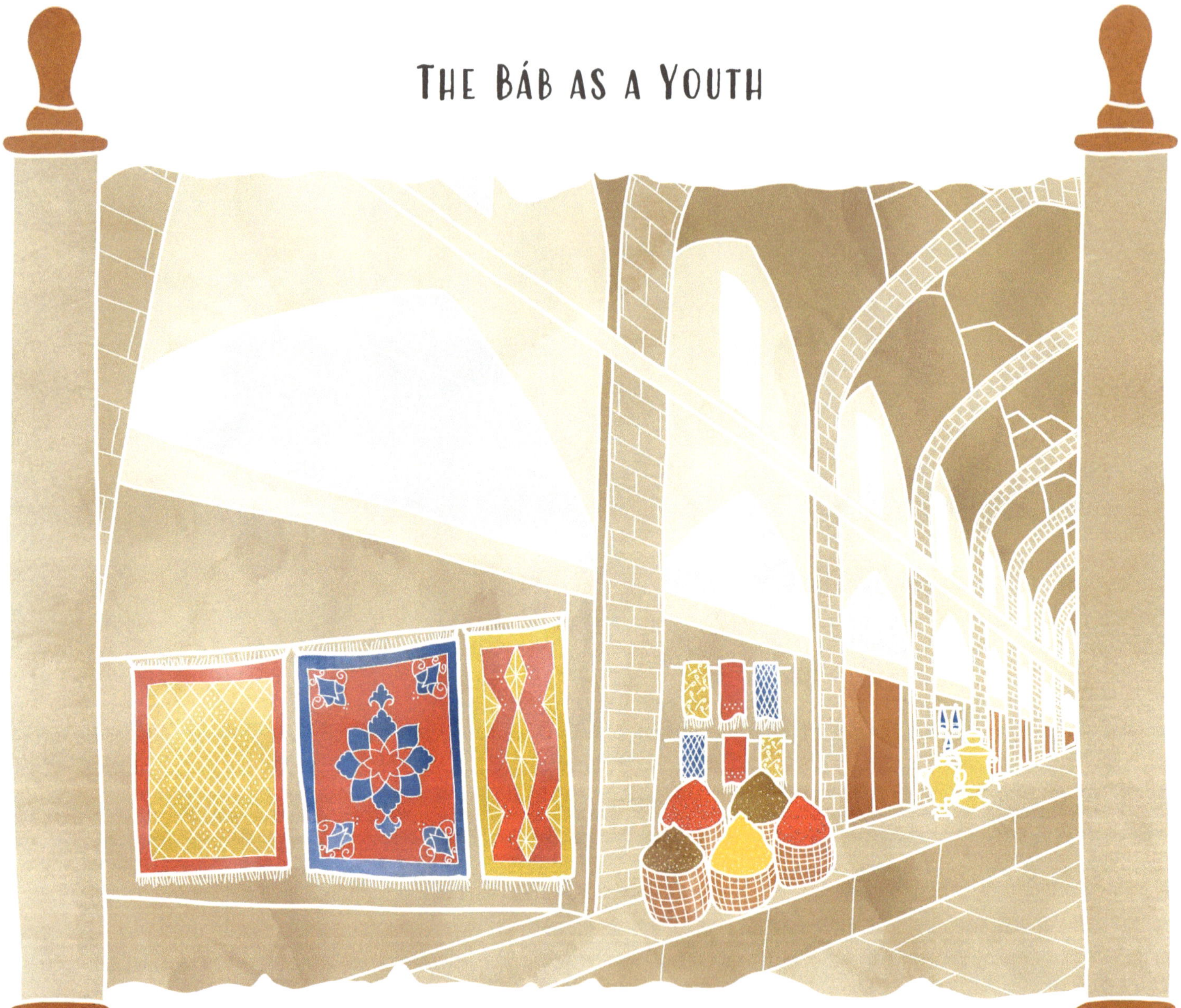

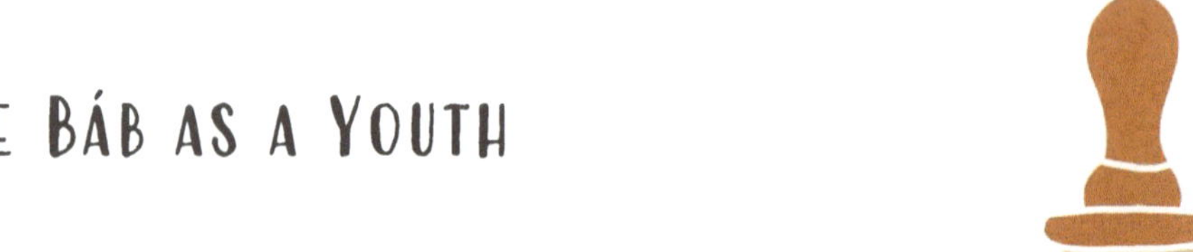

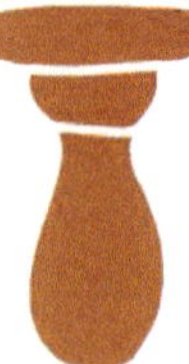

As a youth, the Báb learned the family trade and became an honest and fair merchant, helping His uncles with the family business in the city of Bú<u>sh</u>ihr, Persia.

Bahá'u'lláh as a Youth

As a youth, Bahá'u'lláh was expected to succeed His father as a minister in the Persian King's court. Instead He dedicated His life to serving the poor and the needy.

The Family of the Báb

The Báb married Khadíjih-Bagum in 1842.
They had one child named Aḥmad, who died when he was still a baby.

The Holy Family of Bahá'u'lláh

Bahá'u'lláh married Ásíyih Khánum, known as Navváb, in 1835. Together they had seven children. Only 3 survived to adulthood: 'Abdu'l-Bahá, Bahíyyih Khánum, and Mírzá Mihdí. They are known as the Bahá'í Holy Family.

The Báb Becomes Aware of His Station

One night in 1843, the Báb had a dream. During the dream He drank
a few drops of blood from a Muslim martyr. After waking up, the Báb knew in
His heart that God had revealed to Him that He was a Manifestation of God.

Bahá'u'lláh Becomes Aware of His Station

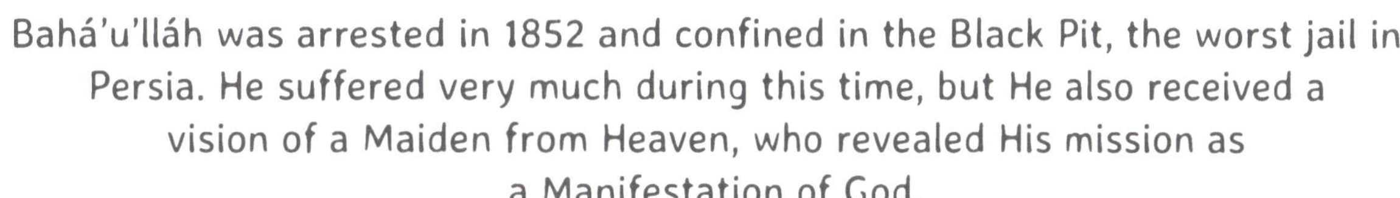

Bahá'u'lláh was arrested in 1852 and confined in the Black Pit, the worst jail in Persia. He suffered very much during this time, but He also received a vision of a Maiden from Heaven, who revealed His mission as a Manifestation of God.

The Heralds of the Báb

All Divine Manifestations are announced by a herald. The Báb's coming was announced by two Muslim teachers: first, <u>Shaykh</u> Aḥmad and later, Siyyid Káẓim. They prepared their students to look for the Promised One of the Qur'án: the Báb.

The Herald of Bahá'u'lláh

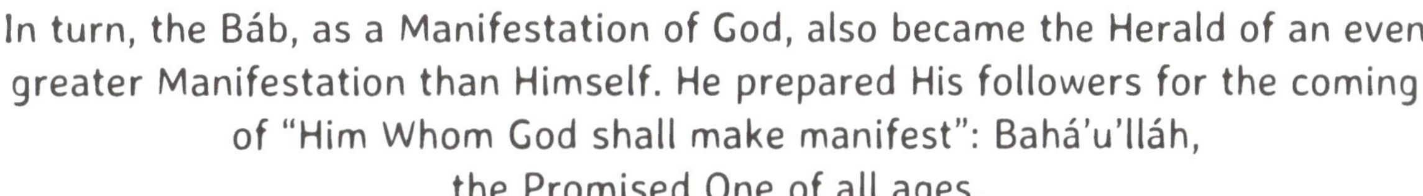

In turn, the Báb, as a Manifestation of God, also became the Herald of an even greater Manifestation than Himself. He prepared His followers for the coming of "Him Whom God shall make manifest": Bahá'u'lláh, the Promised One of all ages.

The Declaration of the Báb

The Báb declared His mission as a Manifestation of God to Mullá Ḥusayn in <u>Sh</u>íráz, Persia, on May 22nd, 1844.

The Declaration of Bahá'u'lláh

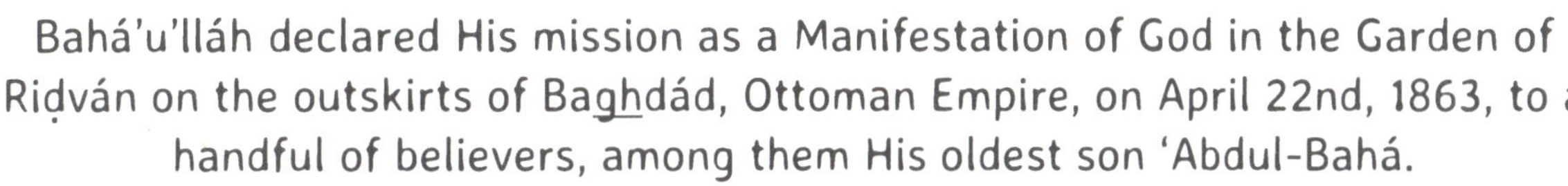

Bahá'u'lláh declared His mission as a Manifestation of God in the Garden of Riḍván on the outskirts of Baghdád, Ottoman Empire, on April 22nd, 1863, to a handful of believers, among them His oldest son 'Abdul-Bahá.

The Bábí Faith

With His declaration, the Báb founded a new religion: the Bábí Faith.

The Bahá'í Faith

With His declaration, Bahá'u'lláh founded a new religion: the Bahá'í Faith.

The Proclamation of the Faith of the Báb

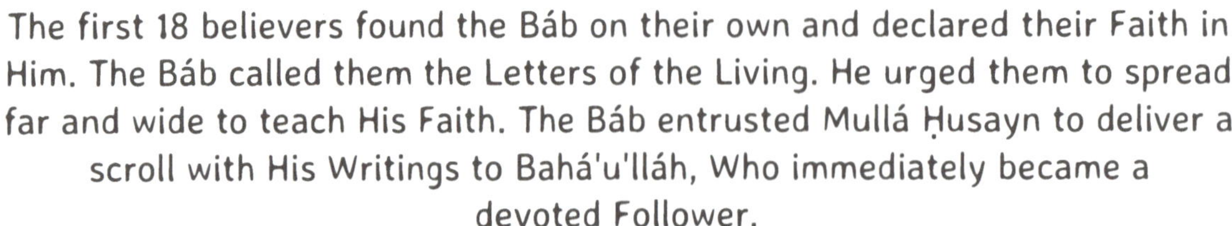

The first 18 believers found the Báb on their own and declared their Faith in Him. The Báb called them the Letters of the Living. He urged them to spread far and wide to teach His Faith. The Báb entrusted Mullá Ḥusayn to deliver a scroll with His Writings to Bahá'u'lláh, Who immediately became a devoted Follower.

The Proclamation of the Faith of Bahá'u'lláh

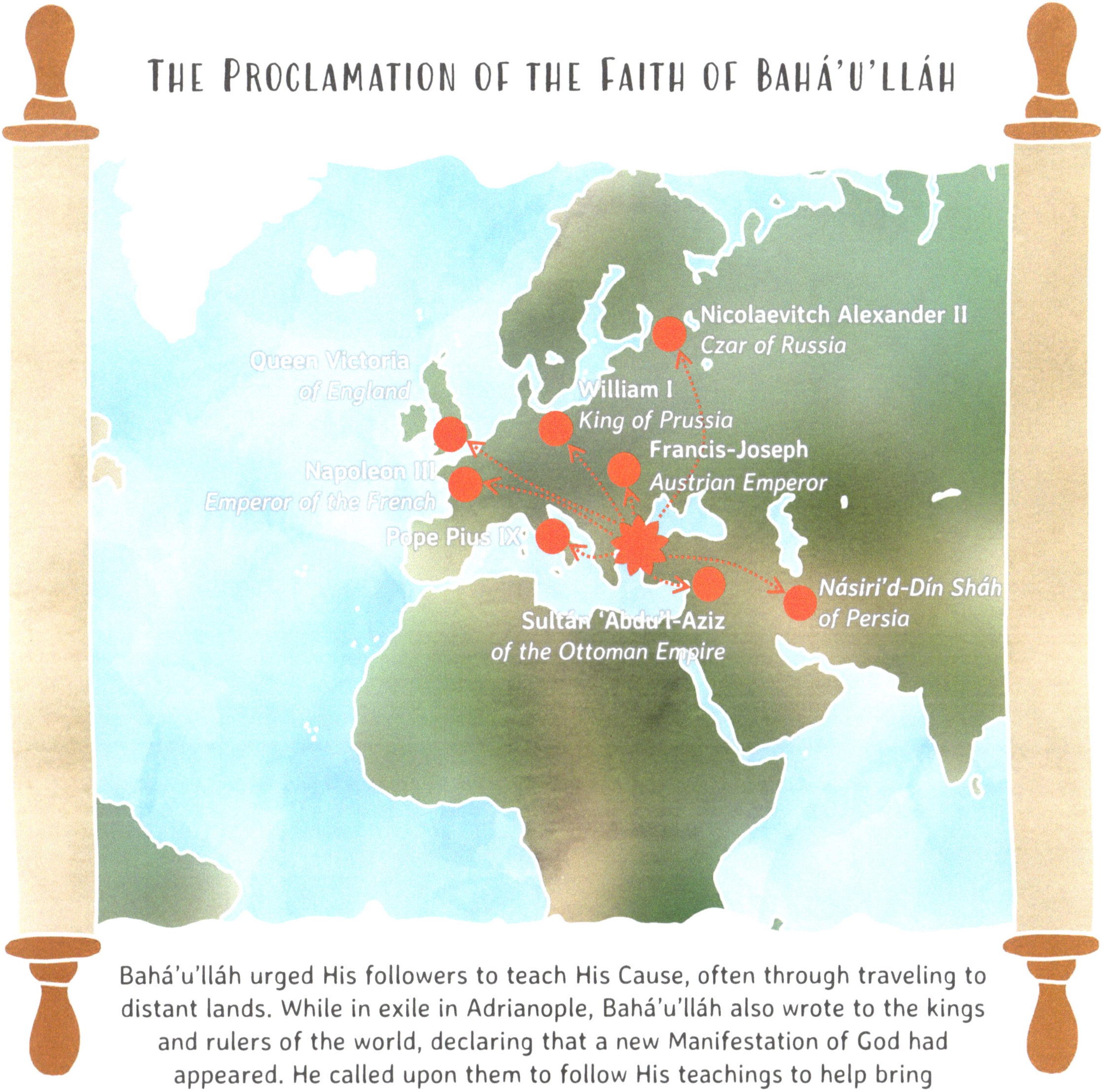

Bahá'u'lláh urged His followers to teach His Cause, often through traveling to distant lands. While in exile in Adrianople, Bahá'u'lláh also wrote to the kings and rulers of the world, declaring that a new Manifestation of God had appeared. He called upon them to follow His teachings to help bring about world peace, yet they rejected or ignored His message.

The Followers of the Báb

The followers of the Báb were called Bábís. At the time of the Declaration of Bahá'u'lláh there were Bábís throughout Persia, India and in some cities of the Ottoman Empire.

The Followers of Bahá'u'lláh

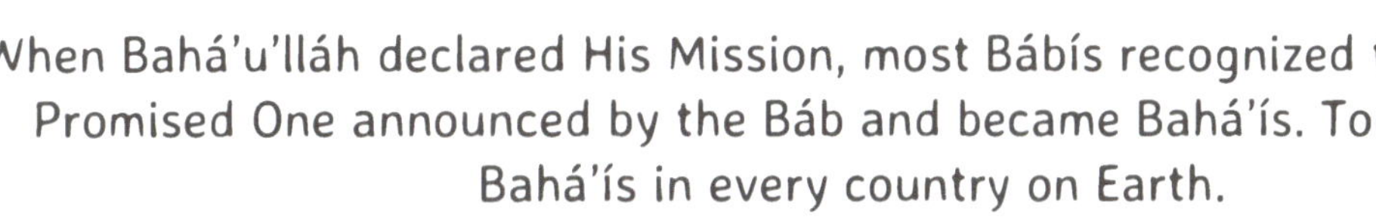

When Bahá'u'lláh declared His Mission, most Bábís recognized that He was the Promised One announced by the Báb and became Bahá'ís. Today there are Bahá'ís in every country on Earth.

The Enemies of the Báb and His Faith

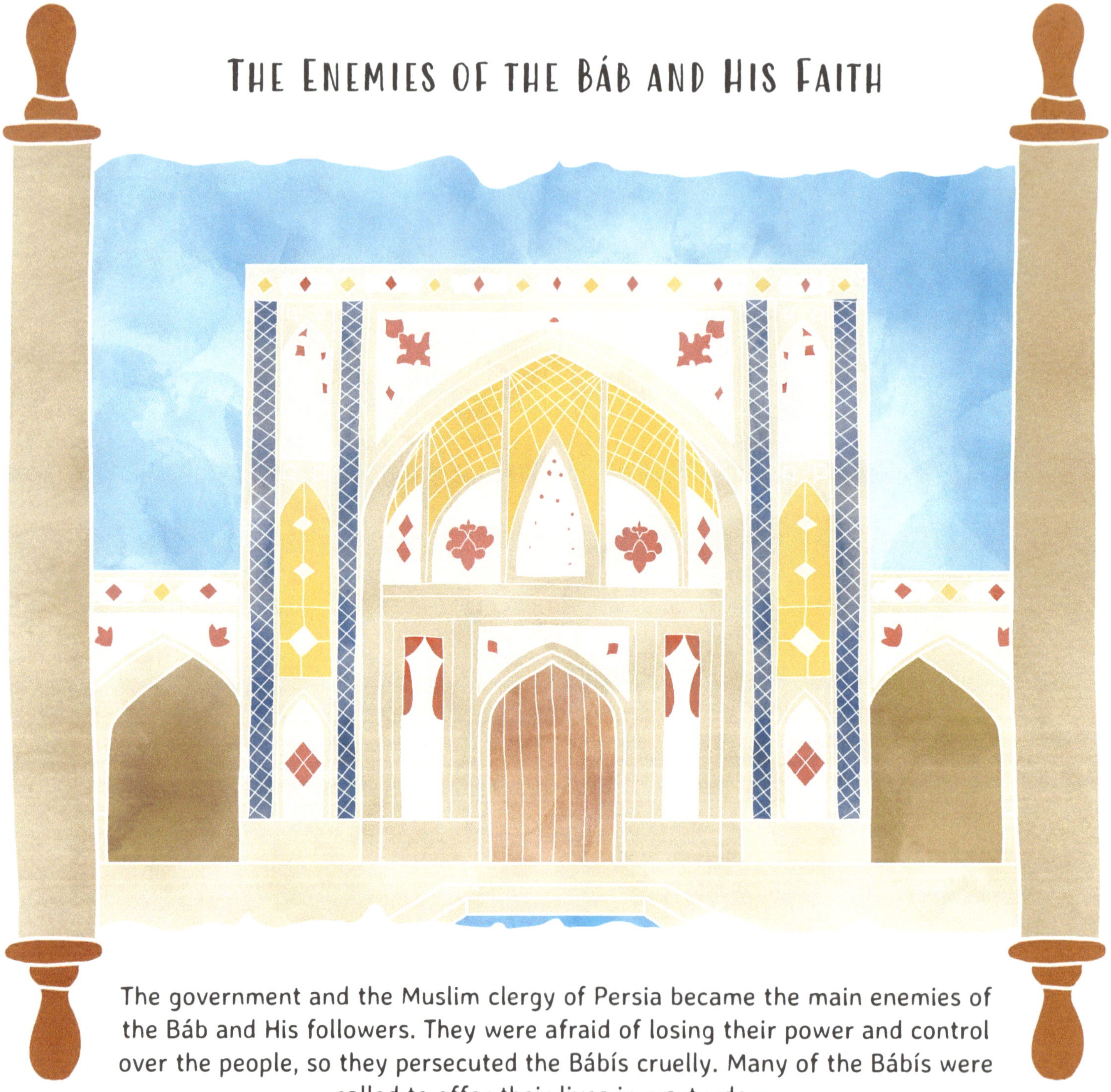

The government and the Muslim clergy of Persia became the main enemies of the Báb and His followers. They were afraid of losing their power and control over the people, so they persecuted the Bábís cruelly. Many of the Bábís were called to offer their lives in martyrdom.

The Enemies of Bahá'u'lláh and His Faith

Bahá'u'lláh's half brother, Mirza Yaḥyá, was an internal enemy who brought great shame to the Faith. The government and the Muslim clergy of Persia continued to be the main external enemies of Bahá'u'lláh and His followers. However, the Ottoman Empire also became a powerful enemy of the Faith. Even now, Bahá'ís in the Middle East are often deprived of basic needs, put in jail, and sometimes called to offer their lives in martyrdom.

The Arrest and Exiles of the Báb

After declaring His mission to the early believers, the Báb went on an Islamic pilgrimage to the holy city of Mecca. On His return to Persia, the government arrested Him in the city of Shíráz and later sent Him to Iṣfahán. The Báb was then imprisoned in various fortresses in the Province of Ádhirbáyján. He was finally sent to the city of Tabríz, where He was martyred.

The Arrest and Exiles of Bahá'u'lláh

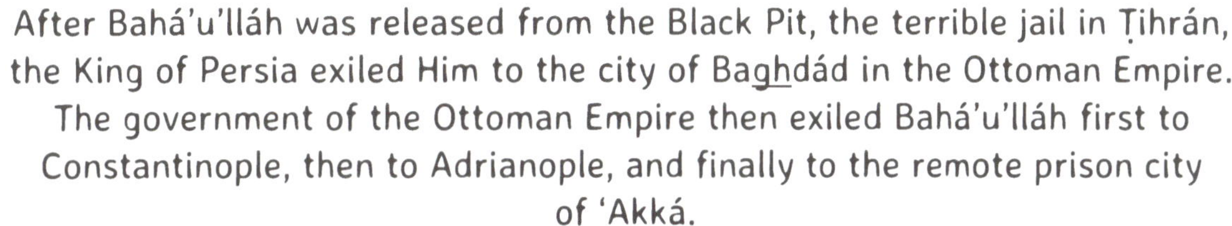

After Bahá'u'lláh was released from the Black Pit, the terrible jail in Ṭihrán, the King of Persia exiled Him to the city of Baghdád in the Ottoman Empire. The government of the Ottoman Empire then exiled Bahá'u'lláh first to Constantinople, then to Adrianople, and finally to the remote prison city of 'Akká.

The Holy Word Revealed by the Báb

During the six years of His mission, the Báb revealed the Word of God in numerous books and tablets, many of which were explanations of the Qur'án and Muslim traditions. His most notable works were the *Persian Bayán* and *Arabic Bayán*, the books containing the spiritual Laws of His Dispensation.

The Holy Word Revealed by Bahá'u'lláh

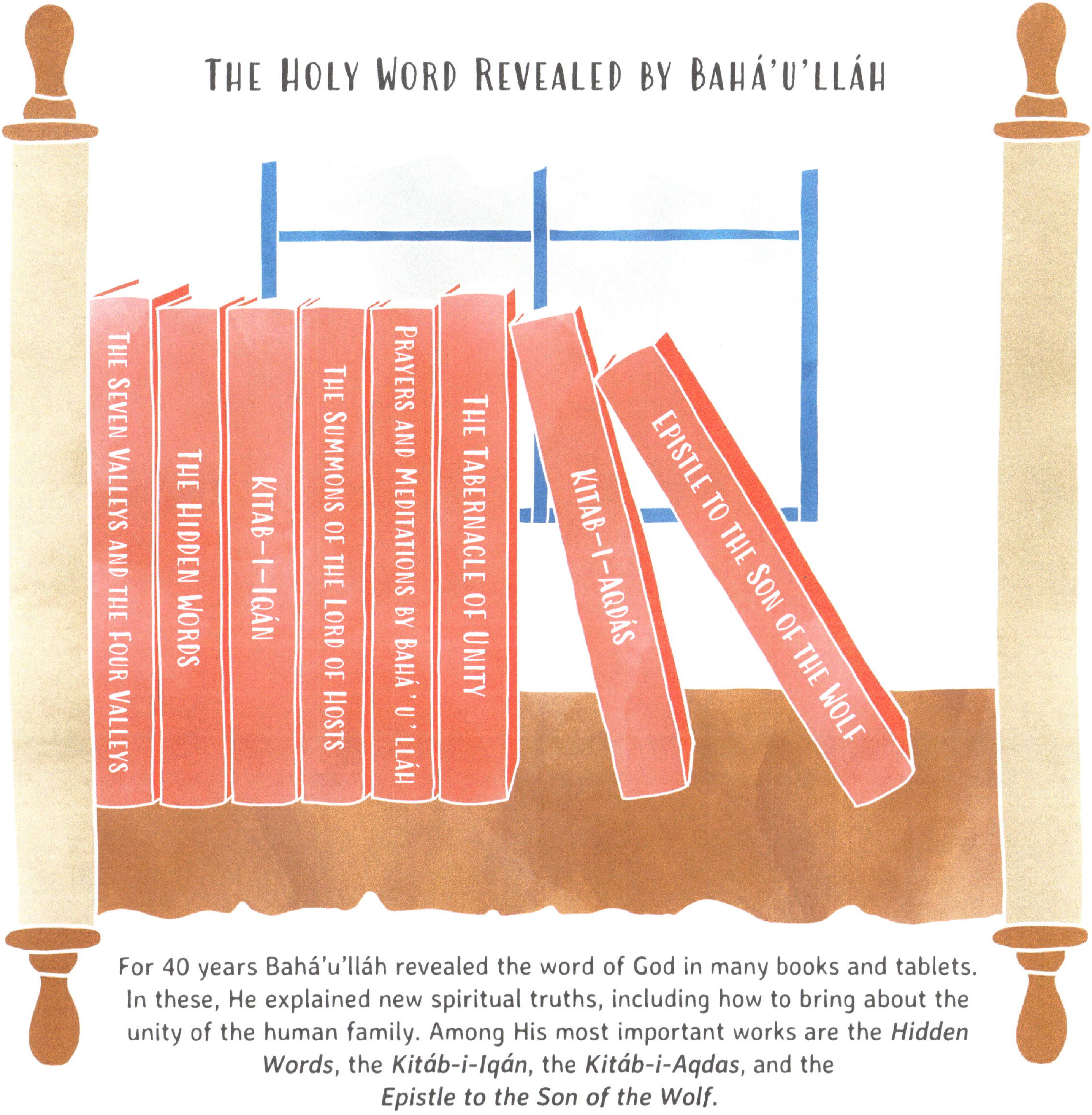

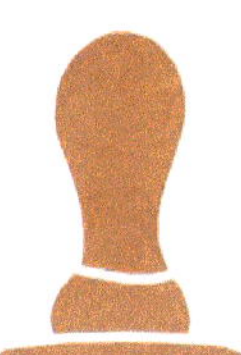

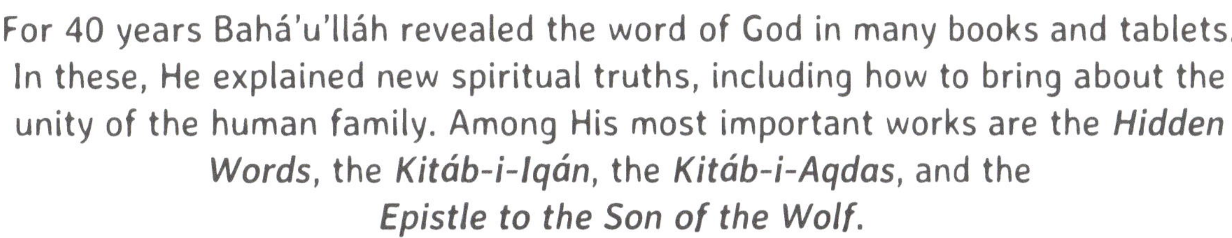

For 40 years Bahá'u'lláh revealed the word of God in many books and tablets. In these, He explained new spiritual truths, including how to bring about the unity of the human family. Among His most important works are the *Hidden Words*, the *Kitáb-i-Iqán*, the *Kitáb-i-Aqdas*, and the *Epistle to the Son of the Wolf*.

Final Arrangements made by the Báb

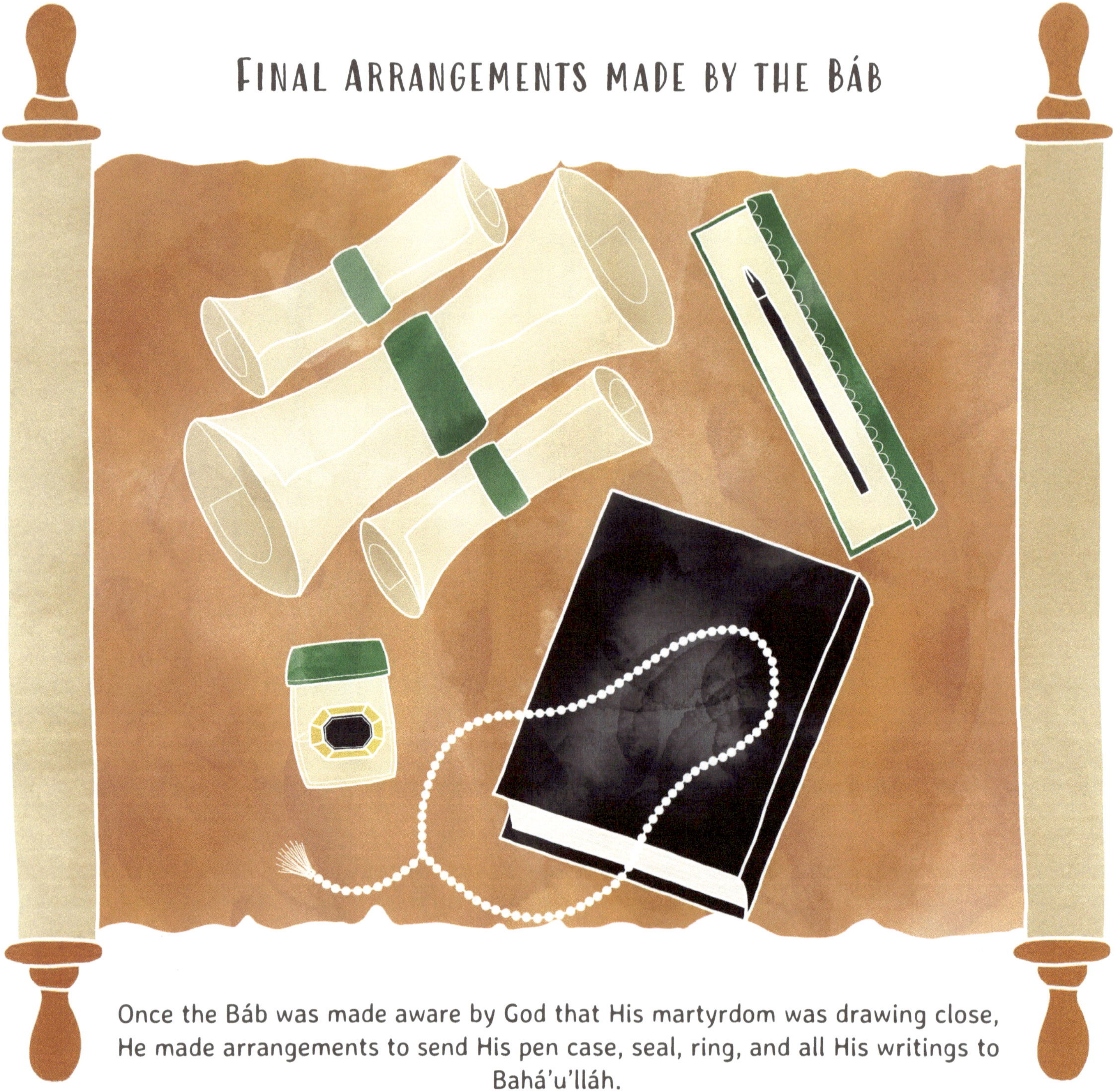

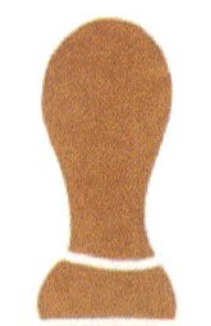

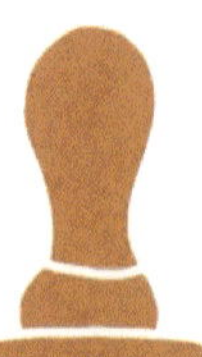

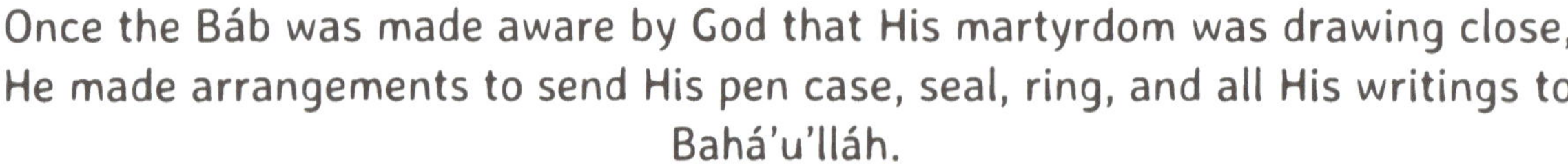

Once the Báb was made aware by God that His martyrdom was drawing close, He made arrangements to send His pen case, seal, ring, and all His writings to Bahá'u'lláh.

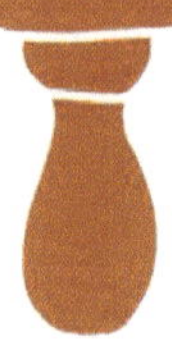

Final Arrangements made by Bahá'u'lláh

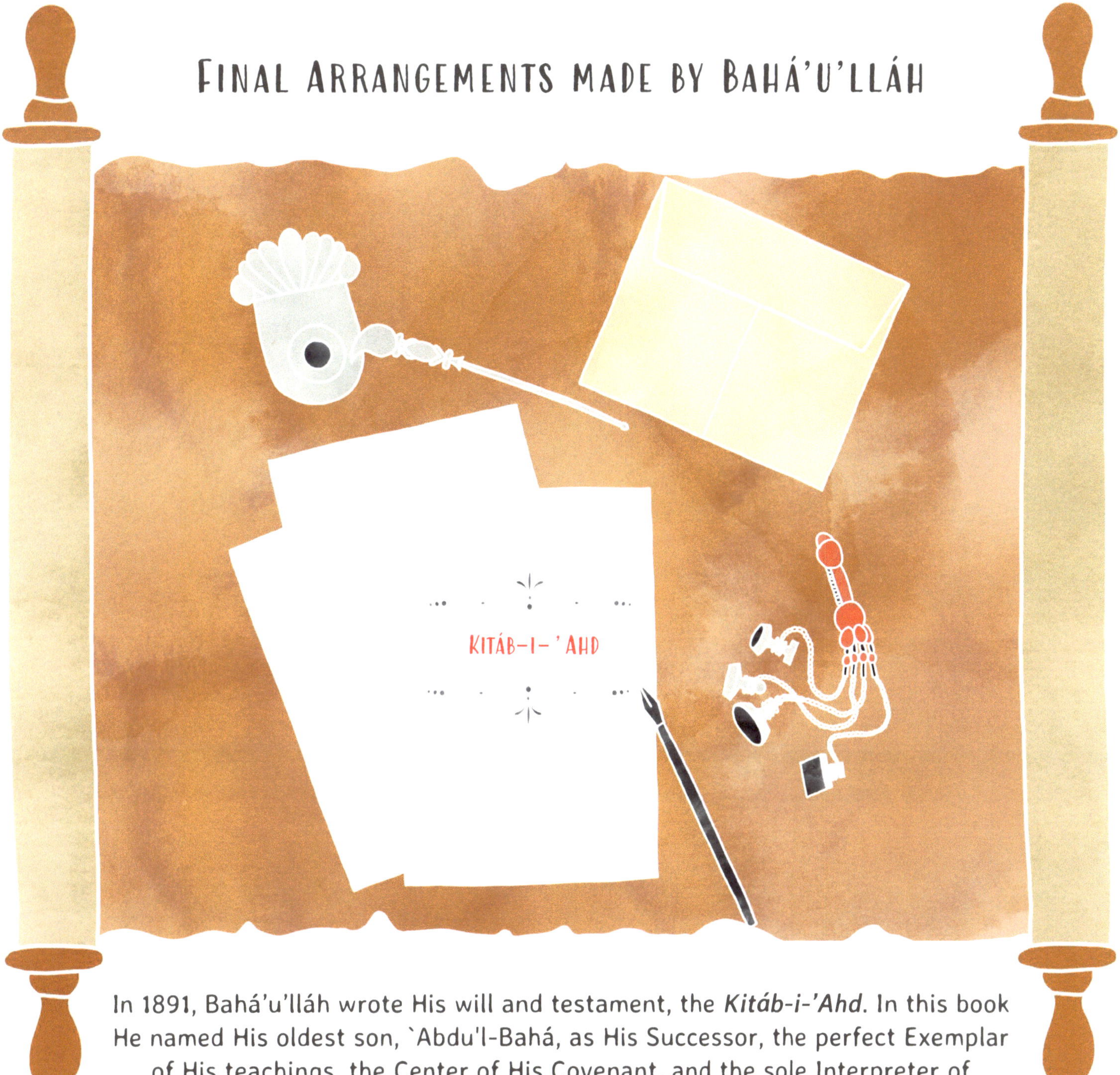

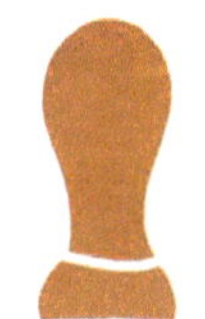

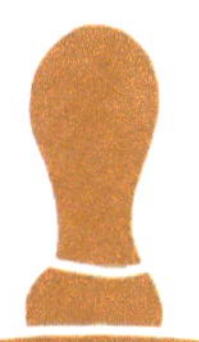

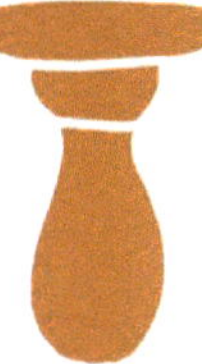

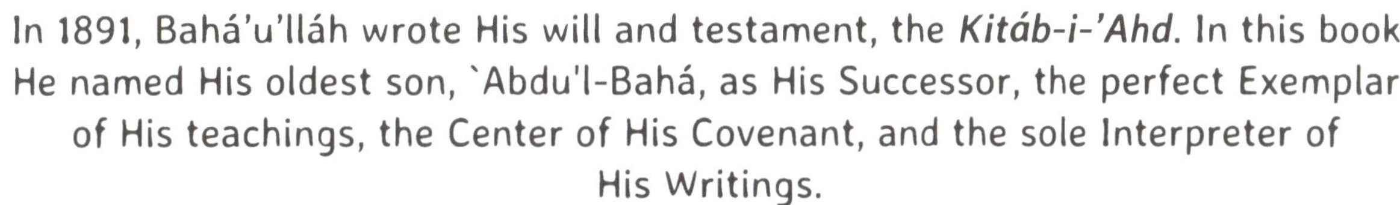

In 1891, Bahá'u'lláh wrote His will and testament, the *Kitáb-i-'Ahd*. In this book He named His oldest son, `Abdu'l-Bahá, as His Successor, the perfect Exemplar of His teachings, the Center of His Covenant, and the sole Interpreter of His Writings.

The Martyrdom of the Báb

The Báb was martyred on July 9th, 1850, in the city of Tabríz, Persia.
He was 30 years old.

The Ascension of Bahá'u'lláh

Bahá'u'lláh passed away in the Mansion of Bahjí in 'Akká, present-day Israel,
on May 29th, 1892. He was 74 years old.

The Shrine of the Báb

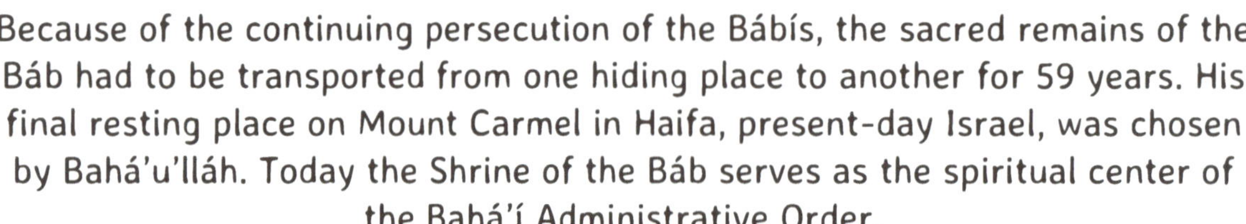

Because of the continuing persecution of the Bábís, the sacred remains of the Báb had to be transported from one hiding place to another for 59 years. His final resting place on Mount Carmel in Haifa, present-day Israel, was chosen by Bahá'u'lláh. Today the Shrine of the Báb serves as the spiritual center of the Bahá'í Administrative Order.

The Shrine of Bahá'u'lláh

The sacred remains of Bahá'u'lláh were buried in the house next to the Mansion of Bahjí. This hallowed spot is the Qiblih - or point of adoration- for Bahá'ís around the world. Bahá'ís turn to face the Qiblih during special prayers, such as the Obligatory Prayer.

The Báb founded a new religion and prepared humanity for "Him Whom God shall make manifest."

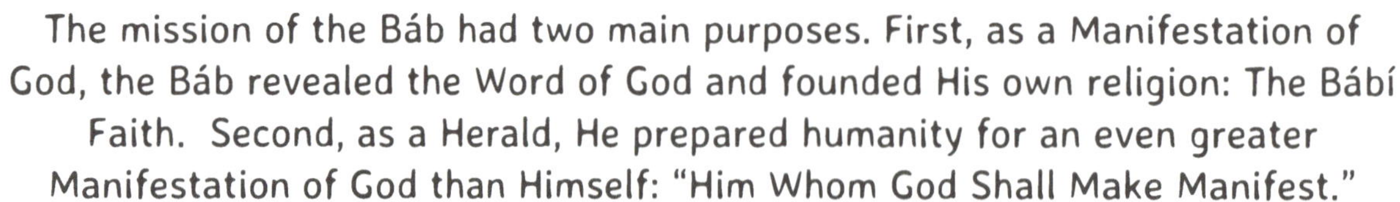

The mission of the Báb had two main purposes. First, as a Manifestation of God, the Báb revealed the Word of God and founded His own religion: The Bábí Faith. Second, as a Herald, He prepared humanity for an even greater Manifestation of God than Himself: "Him Whom God Shall Make Manifest."

Bahá'u'lláh founded a new religion and taught humanity about the oneness of God, the oneness of religion, and the oneness of Humanity.

Bahá'u'lláh was the Manifestation of God promised by the Báb. His mission was to teach us about the oneness of God, the oneness of religion, and the oneness of humanity, which will bring about world unity.

The Life of the Báb
General Timeline

October 20, 1819	Birth of the Báb (Date equal to 1st of Muḥarram 1235 A.H.)
1835-1836	The Báb moves to Búshihr to manage His uncles' business
1841	The Báb goes to Karbilá, where He occasionally attends the lectures of Siyyid Kázim
August 1842	Marriage of the Báb to Khadíjih-Bagum
January 10, 1843	The Báb has a dream where God reveals that He is a Manifestation of God
May 22, 1844	Declaration of the Báb's Mission to Mullá Ḥusayn
Sept. – Oct. 1844	The Báb receives word from Mullá Ḥusayn that he has delivered the scroll to Bahá'u'lláh
1844—1845	The Báb's pilgrimage to Mecca and Medina
June 1845	The Báb is arrested in Shiráz
September 24, 1846	The Báb is exiled to Iṣfahán
April 1847	The King orders the Báb to go to the fortress of Máh-Kú in Ádhirbáyján
1848	The Báb reveals the *Persian Bayán* and the *Arabic Bayán*
April 10, 1848	The Báb is transferred to the fortress of Chihríq
July 1848	Trial of the Báb
August 1848	The Báb is taken back to Chihríq
June 1850	The Báb arranges for His documents, Tablets, pen case, seal, and ring to be delivered to Bahá'u'lláh
July 8, 1850	The Báb is transported back to Tabríz
July 9, 1850	Martyrdom of the Báb in Tabriz
1850– 1909	Transportation of the sacred remains of the Báb to various hiding places
March 21, 1909	Interment of the sacred remains in the Shrine in Haifa by `Abdu'l-Bahá

The Life of the Bahá'u'lláh
General Timeline

November 12, 1817	Birth of Bahá'u'lláh (Date equal to 2nd of Muḥarram 1233 A.H.)
October 1835	Marriage of Bahá'u'lláh to Navváb
1839	Passing of Mírzá Buzurg. Bahá'u'lláh is offered his position in the Persian King's court but rejects it
1844	Bahá'u'lláh receives the scroll from the Báb and becomes a Bábí
1844	Bahá'u'lláh teaches the Faith of the Báb in His native province of Mázindarán
1848	Bahá'u'lláh serves as one of the hosts for the Conference of Badasht
Aug - Dec 1852	Following an attempt on the life of the King by several misguided Bábís, Bahá'u'lláh is arrested and taken to the Black Pit. There He receives a vision that He is a Manifestation of God
1853-1863	Bahá'u'lláh is exiled to Baghdád
April – May 1863	Declaration of Bahá'u'lláh during His stay in the Garden of Riḍván outside Baghdád
May - Dec 1863	Bahá'u'lláh is exiled to Constantinople
1867	Bahá'u'lláh reveals the *Súriy-Mulúk*, the *Tablet to the Kings*
1863-1868	Bahá'u'lláh is exiled to Adrianople
1868	Bahá'u'lláh is exiled to `Akká
October 1870	Bahá'u'lláh is allowed to leave the prison
1873	Bahá'u'lláh reveals the *Kitáb-i-Aqdas*
May 29, 1892	The Ascension of Bahá'u'lláh in the Mansion of Bahjí. His sacred remains are buried in the house next to the Mansion

THE LIFE OF THE BÁB
Illustration Index

For further information about the Bahá'í Faith, please visit:

WWW.BAHAI.ORG

REFERENCES

`Abdu'l-Bahá, *Memorials of the Faithful*

Adib Taherzadeh, *The Revelation of Bahá'u'lláh*

Baharieh Rouhani Ma'ani, *Leaves of the Twin Divine Trees*

Bahá'í World Centre, *Visiting Bahá'í Holy Places*

Bahá'u'lláh, *Gleanings from the Writings of Bahá'u'lláh*

Bahá'u'lláh, *Tabernacle of Unity*

Bahá'u'lláh, *Bahá'í Prayers*

Bahá'u'lláh, *Epistle to the Son of the Wolf*

Bahá'u'lláh, *Tablets of Bahá'u'lláh*

Bahá'u'lláh, *Tablet of Carmel*

Bahá'u'lláh, *Kitáb-i-Aqdas*

Earl Redman, *'Abdu'l-Baha in Their Midst*

Frances Worthington, *Abraham One God Three Wives Five Religions*

Helen Bassett Hornby, *Lights of Guidance*

H.M. Balyuzi, *Bahá'u'lláh: the King of Glory*

H.M. Balyuzi, *The Báb*

Janet A. Khan, *Prophet's Daughter*

J. E. Esslemont, *Bahá'u'lláh and the New Era*

Kaiser Barnes, *Stories of Bahá'u'lláh and Other Notable Believers*

Michael V. Day, *Journey to a Mountain*

Oxford Dictionary

Ruhi Institute, *Book 4: The Twin Manifestations*

Shoghi Effendi, *God Passes By*

Shoghi Effendi, *The Dawn-Breakers: Nabíl's Narrative of the Early Days of the Bahá'í Revelation*

Shoghi Effendi, *The World Order of Bahá'u'lláh*

Shoghi Effendi, *The Promised Day is Come*

The Báb, *Selections from the Writings of the Báb*

Heartfelt Thanks to:

My beloved husband Darioush Charepoo for all his support.
Our dearly loved boys for being the inspiration.
Leanna Guillén Mora for helping with proofreading and editing the book.

www.ingramcontent.com/pod-product-compliance
Lightning Source LLC
Chambersburg PA
CBHW042151030726
47599CB00004B/698